Enliven Your

RelationshiP

INTELLECTUALLY ANIMATING GAMES.
EVALUATE EACH OTHER
TRUST AND RESPONSIBILITY
SEX AND CLOSENESS

ALEX RICHARD

TABLE OF CONTENTS

INTRODUCTION

Close connections emerge from couples getting to know one another on numerous various levels. While many couples treat physical and close to home closeness as necessities, they may effectively push scholarly closeness to the wayside. This can demonstrate lamentable, as knowing and adoring your accomplice on a scholarly level can assist with extending your association like never before previously.

WHAT IS SCHOLARLY CLOSENESS?

Scholarly closeness is the scholarly association between two individuals in a heartfelt connection. To share closeness of any kind, individuals need to feel they can be their actual selves around their life partner. On a scholarly level, this implies feeling glad to openly impart insights about recent developments, appreciate comparative types of diversion, or figure out how to do new things together.

ADVANTAGES OF SCHOLARLY CLOSENESS

Scholarly closeness helps fabricate an establishment for effective connections. Here are only three vital advantages to expect when you become all the more mentally private with your accomplice:

✧ MORE PROMINENT SCHOLARLY EXCITEMENT

The two players in a relationship stand to acquire from scholarly closeness on a simply individual level. Assuming that you and your accomplice share similar interests, it's far simpler to invigorate each other on a scholarly plane than if you had no shared conviction.

✧ EXPANDED ASSOCIATION

Despite the fact that scholarly closeness could sound very cerebral, it can achieve a broad level of profound closeness also. It can assist with working on your emotional well-being and neutralize any frailties you could have since you'll foster more noteworthy certainty as you see an individual you love viewing your contemplations and interests in a serious way. This shared feeling of adoration and regard is fundamental for any solid relationship.

✧ MORE NORMAL GROUND

The more things you share in like manner, the more open doors you need to make a sensation of wellbeing and security for your accomplice. Individuals feel calm around other people who see the world in generally the same manner as they do. This can help both of you move past any remaining anxiety toward closeness and further develop the prosperity of your relationship.

CHAPTER ONE

SPICE THINGS UP ON A SCHOLARLY LEVEL WITH YOUR ACCOMPLICE?

Carefully captivating your accomplice is smart for your relationship, and it will give it the launch it needs on the off chance that you're trapped in an endless cycle.

✧ MAKE A RUNDOWN OF INTRIGUING SUBJECTS

Request that your accomplice make a comparable rundown, then, at that point, trade records. Consistently, pick a subject of discussion from your accomplice's rundown and examination and read about it for 10 to 30 minutes and read it. Next time you and your soul mate are during supper or riding in the vehicle, wow them with your recently tracked down information about their inclinations - be prepared to pose inquiries as well. After the primary discussion ceases to exist (in the event that it does), trade subjects.

- **TALK ABOUT MOTION PICTURES IN THE WAKE OF WATCHING THEM.**

Try not to allow your film to encounter end in the cinema. Go for a 20-minute stroll and discuss it. Pose each other inquiries, for example, Did you like it? What was your #1 and least main thing? Most loved character? Most loved line? Did you like the completion? What might you have done any other way? Investigate thoughts together.

- **PLAY INTELLECTUALLY ANIMATING GAMES.**

Play: What's your #1... would you rather... how might you respond... in the event that you were stuck on a remote location... and so on. Also, get odd with it!

For instance: Assuming you tumbled from the realm state building, how about you kick the bucket on the off chance that you were an insect? It appears to be immature, however it's great to interface with that side around the individual we trust the most. Let it all out!

Try not to stall out with your obligations and become serious. Make sure to play as a team.

✧ PICK A POINT FOR A STORY.

Have one individual make up the start of the story. Then, at that point, you or your accomplice makes up the following sentence of the story. Keep alternating, making up each line for the story, until you have this ludicrously entertaining story. This exercise will get both of your imaginative energies pumping and could motivate you to have one more theme for discussion.

✧ EVALUATE EACH OTHER'S SIDE INTERESTS.

How does your accomplice get a kick out of the chance to help fun? Request to attempt it with them, and permit them to show you how it functions. One week from now, acquaint them with one of your side interests.

✧ HELP EACH OTHER WITH PROJECTS.

Is your sweetheart structure a bird enclosure? Snatch a sledge and propose to help out. Is your significant other dealing with a little robot? Volunteer to assist her test it and watch it with going. This offers you the chance to gain from your companion, and comprehend the things that make them light up.

✧ PICK NEW ACTIVITIES TOGETHER.

Request your accomplice to compose a rundown from things they've for practically forever needed to attempt, and think of one yourself. Then make a rundown of things to attempt as a team. Consider spots to go, food sources to attempt, exercises to explore different avenues regarding, and whatever else rings a bell.

Ponder the things you see as energizing.

Be imaginative and expand upon the original encounters you partook in when you got together interestingly.

- **ASSIGN ONE DAY OF THE WEEK TO GO OUT TOGETHER.**

Visit a historical center, ocean side, aquarium, café, or anything that intrigues you two. This will make going out and getting to know each other a daily practice.

- **MAKE TIME CONSISTENTLY TO CONVERSE WITH YOUR ACCOMPLICE.**

Correspondence is one of the main parts of a relationship; don't make everything about food and tasks. Have a good time in your discussions, anticipate chatting with one another, and watch your relationship develop. Be the one your accomplice goes to for scholarly excitement. You and your accomplice will have some good times re-associating, adoring, and getting to know one another once more.

Remember that quiet isn't generally something terrible. It's OK to sit for some time peacefully, or simply partake in an energetic kiss. You don't need to continually be mentally "on" to partake in a superb relationship.

CHAPTER TWO

THE DISCUSSIONS THAT MAKE THE BIGGEST DIFFERENCE IN CONNECTIONS

A few discussions matter more than others in connections.

You associate and experience passionate feelings for by talking. In any case, what discussions would it be advisable for you to have with your accomplice to be aware assuming your adoration will endure — through challenges, astonishments, delight, and agony?

Furthermore, on the off chance that you've been seeing someone years, what discussions would it be a good idea for you to need to revitalize the association and enthusiasm that initially united you, however may have become everyday practice?

Offering enabling ways of finding the adoration you need and merit, this widely tried program of eight tomfoolery, discussion based dates will bring about a long period of understanding and responsibility, whether you're recently infatuated or have been together for a really long time.

Since a blissful relationship isn't the consequence of sharing bunches of things for all intents and purpose — as we frequently suspect. It comes from knowing how to address your center distinctions such that upholds each other's necessities and dreams.

✧ TRUST AND RESPONSIBILITY

Trust is treasuring one another and showing your accomplice that you can be relied on. Picking responsibility implies tolerating your accomplice precisely as the person in question is, notwithstanding their blemishes.

✧ STRUGGLE

Struggle occurs in each relationship, and it's a fantasy to accept that in a cheerful relationship you'll get along constantly. Relationship struggle fills a need. It's an amazing chance to get to realize your accomplice better and to foster further closeness as you discuss and deal with your disparities.

✧ SEX AND CLOSENESS

Heartfelt, close ceremonies of association keep a relationship blissful and energetic. Couples who discuss sex have more sex, however discussing sex is hard for most of couples — it gets simpler and more agreeable the more you make it happen.

✧ WORK AND CASH

Cash issues aren't about cash. They're about how cash affects each accomplice in a relationship. Finding what cash means to both of you will go quite far in settling the struggles you might have around cash.

✧ FAMILY

Roughly 66% of couples have a sharp drop in relationship fulfillment not long after a kid is conceived, and this drop gets further with each ensuing kid. To keep away from this drop in relationship bliss, struggle should be low and you really want to keep up with your sexual relationship.

✧ TOMFOOLERY AND EXPERIENCE

Play and experience are indispensable parts to a fruitful and euphoric relationship. It's OK assuming you and your accomplice have various thoughts regarding what is play and experience. The key is for you to regard each other's feeling of experience and how it affects that accomplice.

✧ DEVELOPMENT AND OTHERWORLDLINESS

The main consistent in a relationship is change. The key is the manner by which every individual in the relationship obliges the development of the other accomplice. Connections can be something other than two people meeting up — they can be accounts of change and incredible commitment and importance to the world.

✧ DREAMS

Respecting each other's fantasies is the mysterious fixing to making love for a lifetime. At the point when dreams are regarded, all the other things in the relationship gets more straightforward.

Each solid relationship is a consequence of a ceaseless discussion between accomplices.

CHAPTER THREE

POINTS TO BUILD YOUR RELATIONSHIP

Correspondence unites darlings and makes it simple for them to construct science and love. The discussions you have with your life partner assume areas of strength for an in deciding how blissful, fun and solid your relationship will be.

Regardless of how troublesome a few subjects might appear some of the time, examining them will assist with facilitating a great deal of strain and pass on space for your relationship to develop. You'll likewise find that you both see each other better.

It doesn't make any difference whether you are in another relationship or you've been hitched for a really long time. These themes won't just assist you with drawing nearer to your darling; it will likewise give you thoughts on what to discuss when it seems like you are running out of subjects. Furthermore, you can continuously refine and rehash them as you and your accomplice will constantly have various responses each opportunity they come up. Along these lines, you won't ever run out of fascinating discussions.

- **PLANS FOR THE END OF THE WEEK (OR A GET-AWAY)**

It doesn't make any difference whether it's a baffling Monday night or Thursday night. Discussing your arrangements for the end of the week and you'll both have something invigorating to anticipate. It will likewise persuade you to work and traverse the week with much energy. Preparing of time for a get-away or that little escape likewise gives you the two things to examine and ponder on. So anticipate!

✧ WORK

A straightforward "how did things turn out" and a fair response can prompt a discussion you will both treasure. What's more, there is continuously something to discuss work. From an odd partner to a terrible supervisor to the undertakings you need to finish, these discussions will help you both see each other's expert sides better.

✧ SEX

Sexual closeness is pretty much as significant as heartfelt signals. Discuss what turns you on, the positions or toys you might want to attempt, your physically delicate spots, your mystery dreams and each and every other thing connected with sex. This will both be invigorating and uncovering simultaneously, and you'll wind up finding new things about one another. Be that as it may, this additionally remembers issues for bed. Shout out about them or they will ultimately pivot and mess with you toward the back. In the event that your accomplice isn't proceeding true to form or your sex drive has decreased definitely, discuss it. Consider or recommend better approaches for dealing with it together and you will be one stage towards conquering these issues.

✧ OFFER PRAISES

Tell your accomplice the things you like about them. Make a propensity for valuing their character or seemingly insignificant details they did the other day, even the ones they didn't understand that they were doing. Valuing individuals urges them to accomplish more.

✧ STRESSES

What is annoying or concerning you? Basic inquiry, correct? However, this is the sort of thing that will cause your accomplice to feel adored and really focused on.

They might have not a care in the world, however the prospect that you care will cause them to treasure being involved with you. Likewise discuss medical problems, whether they are not difficult to make reference to.

✧ INSIDER FACTS

It is fun, disclosing yet enjoyable to Discuss privileged insights. You can transform it into a game where you each uncover another grimy, minimal mystery. It will assist you with getting to know one another personally.

✧ SHOWS AND FILMS

Indeed, this generally gives you something to discuss. New shows and motion pictures come out each week. Watch one together and discuss it. Giggle at them for crying when Mufasa passed on while you watched Lion Lord once more.

✧ THE FUTURE AND THE PAST

The past may not generally be fun and invigorating to discuss, however there will certainly be comical minutes to make reference to, similar to the times you did senseless things as a kid or your experience growing up dreams. You don't have to discuss difficult recollections like past connections or delve into sexual subtleties. Discuss your arrangements for what's to come: the objectives you have, your fantasies, goals and life pursuits. Let them know what you mean to do. This will help the both of you see each other's perspectives. Discuss where you consider yourselves to be a couple in five years. Make objectives that will ask you both to pursue reinforcing your relationship.

✧ PLACES

Discuss your #1 eateries, that bukka you just found in the following road, a fantasy area you coincidentally found on the web, places you might want to visit over the course of the end of the week or on unique days, or a cool spot you could both sit quietly or make out in. It will allow you both the opportunity to investigate these spots together.

✧ INDIVIDUAL INTERESTS

What do you really appreciate doing? Share these contemplations with your accomplice and see which interests struggle and which ones supplement each other. At the point when these interests complete one another, have a go at doing them together as it will bring you closer.

✧ LOVED ONES

Knowing (about) your accomplice's companions makes you a stride nearer to diving deeper into them. Likewise, discussing each other's families furnishes you with a really long time of intriguing significance. You might need to stop yourselves deliberately. This likewise makes first acquaintances with loved ones simpler and more tomfoolery.

✧ FEELINGS AND INCLINATIONS

Never keep your contemplations away from somebody you love. Shout out and express your convictions. Discuss each other's preferences. Inclinations and conclusions change with time and new data. The more you are familiar each other's inclinations, the better you are familiar them.

✧ IMPROVEMENT

Discuss your imperfections and the manners in which you might want to move along. Delivering your weaknesses uninhibitedly will assist your band together with loosening up more around you and they will separate their own walls and discuss theirs as well. Give and get exhortation and thoughts on ways you can both work on yourselves.

✧ PROPOSE TO HELP

Propose to assist your cooperate with something, whether or not it is a simple errand or a hard one. Cooperating on an errand unites you. Additionally they will be happy you helped. Discuss ways you can assist them around the house with tasks and housework.

✧ GLAD MINUTES

Request that your accomplice educate you regarding the minutes in life when they've felt truly pleased with their own accomplishments. Essential minutes and cherished, lifelong recollections generally accommodate long periods of tomfoolery, funny discussions.

CHAPTER FOUR

METHOD FOR KEEPING YOUR ADORED ONE INTELLECTUALLY ANIMATED

Ensuring that your cherished one remaining parts intellectually dynamic is pretty much as significant as keeping them genuinely dynamic. Mental decay is certainly not an unavoidable piece of maturing, and mental excitement can keep sicknesses like Alzheimer's and Parkinson's under control.

Two essentials can keep your adored one intellectually solid. Right off the bat, actual activity is a vital piece of remaining areas of strength for intellectually, concentrates on demonstrating the way that exercise can battle Alzheimer's and Parkinson's. Furthermore, diet is significant for keeping up with mental strength. A decent eating regimen, low in immersed fats and high in nutrients and minerals, powers a sound body and brain.

One more fundamentally significant piece of assisting your cherished one with remaining intellectually sound is to offer them consistent mental excitement. This can have many prizes, for example, further developed rest, state of mind and memory, which all amount to a significantly more charming life.

Mental excitement takes many structures. Remaining socially dynamic is essential, as discussion and company is fantastic mental activity. In the event that they are capable, participating in bunch exercises, for example, bunch side interests or occasions with visit gatherings, can likewise be an extraordinary way for your cherished one to keep their psyche new.

In any case, mental feeling should likewise be possible alone. Perusing, composing, paying attention to the radio and music, as well as finishing riddles and games can keep your adored one's mind dynamic. The conceivable outcomes here are enormous and the advantages critical.

We are here to help your adored one carry on with the fullest life, so reach out to the Birdie Care Group through visit, telephone or email for additional direction about keeping your cherished one intellectually animated.

Your job is additionally essential in keeping up with your adored one's psychological well-being. Being there to converse with them, to mess around with, to have a great time and giggle together is a critical piece of the arrangement, as well.

CHAPTER FIVE

WAYS OF IMPROVING YOUR RELATIONSHIP

Whether you've been dating somebody some time, right now live with an accomplice, or are important for a long-hitched couple, you may be looking for ways of bettering the relationship you have.

Dissimilar to occasion romantic tales and lighthearted comedies in which everything is settled after a couple of struggles, keeping up with flourishing connections requires some work. Yet, it doesn't need to be troublesome.

With the everyday routine of obligations and frayed nerves, it's reasonable why managing accomplice issues tumbles to the lower part of your rundown. All simply staying aware of life's liabilities — work, kids, family, companions, neighbors, your home — is burdening, and a considerable lot of us are plain worn out. Particularly during troublesome times, it's more straightforward to abstain from confronting your slowing down relationship or dissolved closeness issues.

There are a couple of dependable strategies that work to further develop connections: be a decent audience, cut out time together, partake in a quality sexual coexistence, and evenly divide those bothersome tasks. While these have been demonstrated powerful by relationship specialists, you can likewise stretch out to these seven startling ways of holding and upgrade your relationship.

PART WAYS

It sounds strange as a method for working on your relationship, yet have some time off from your accomplice. Everybody needs their own space and quality time outside a relationship. Dating and marriage mentors advise us that you merit that space to breathe.

People need time all alone for self-improvement and to keep up with freedom inside the bounds of a relationship. While people thrive, the actual relationship benefits. It's vital to fruitful relationships, as a matter of fact.

Whether that implies perusing alone or taking a mobile in the recreation area, make it happen. Or on the other hand perhaps you need to go to an exercise with a companion.

The result is your accomplice's annoying propensities will set off you less. You'll discover yourself feeling revived and being more persistent. Your extraordinary has opportunity and energy to miss you, as well.

✧ DIFFERENT SHELTERS

you'll carry more to the actual relationship. Venturing endlessly routinely forestalls your time together from becoming lifeless. All things considered, it takes into account interest, additional fascinating discussions, and development. As a result, taking time separated will breathe new live into the relationship dynamic.

✧ FALL ASLEEP SIMULTANEOUSLY

Maybe you've previously perused that most American grown-ups are not getting the seven to eight hours out of every evening of solid rest they need. In any case, did you had any idea about that hitting the sack at various times adversely influences you and your accomplice?

For a better relationship, make a beeline for bed simultaneously. There are evening people and morning people who live on various timetables, and afterward there are the individuals who work in bed while the other is watching Netflix in another room. Whatever the circumstance, synchronize your sleep times.

As indicated by Chris Brantner, a guaranteed rest science mentor, 75% of couples don't hit the sack together, which makes adverse consequences. Those with befuddled rest designs report more clash, less discussion, and have less sex than the people who hit the sack together.

This doesn't give you the thumbs up to jump under the covers and look at your online entertainment while you're both in bed.

✧ BE POWERLESS

At times you need to dig profound to be powerless. "Couples might think that it is astonishing, however assuming every one becomes inquisitive around one's own vulnerable sides, finds them, and afterward is sufficiently valiant to share that weakness, it can assist with making further closeness," prompted Meredith Resnick, LCSW, maker of Shamerecovery.com.

Resnick added, "A vulnerable side doesn't be guaranteed to mean a shortcoming or a shortcoming, but instead a profoundly held conviction around oneself or about how a relationship should function, or how love is communicated. The conviction is so profound, we don't for even a moment acknowledge we have it, thus the term vulnerable side."

WHAT IS AN ILLUSTRATION OF VULNERABLE SIDES IN CONNECTIONS?

According to resnick, "For instance, one accomplice could find that their inclination to obsessively fuss over individuals is really connected with their separation anxiety — controlling the timetable of a friend or family member as an approach to never be distant from everyone else.

"Offering this to an accomplice can be the initial step to changing this example. This ought to be a caring interaction that forms trust, not one that causes disgrace," says Resnick.

✧ MAKE NOVEL ENCOUNTERS

Despite the fact that eating your #1 pizza each Saturday night and consolidating customs in your day to day existence reinforces connections, fatigue creeps in. Subsequently, you ought to make a splash — pepper your daily practice with erratic date evenings and snapshots of tomfoolery.

In the event that daring dates like stone climbing or learning another dialect are not feasible now, might you at any point purchase a trampoline or accomplish something surprising? Perhaps you can track down alternate ways of carrying fervor to your relationship.

Analysts say to zero in on oddity, assortment, and shock. Research shows that following quite a while of intriguing dates, members revived their adoration, and the couples felt nearer.

✧ SHOCK WITH EASILY OVERLOOKED DETAILS

Little signals keep the flash alive and remind your accomplice you are contemplating them. Blissful couples are thoughtful to one another. Giving or electing to assist is an or more. As a matter of fact, thoughtful gestures are strong, and those that are spontaneous will generally fuel by and large prosperity.

- **HONOR YOUR ACCOMPLICE'S WAY TO EXPRESS AFFECTION.**

For instance, they embrace you since they esteem actual touch. You'd be significantly more joyful assuming that they tidied up the lounge or invested more energy away from their work area, since you esteem demonstrations of administration and quality time together. In connections, figure out how you can show your accomplice your adoration such that your accomplice values.

BATTLE BETTER

While no one needs to contend with somebody they love, conflicts are, as a matter of fact, solid. It's the manner by which you battle, and assuming you battle reasonably and valuably, that is important.

✧ SOFTEN THE BEGINNING UP

The accentuation is on your tone and aim. Talk delicately and tenderly. Good manners goes quite far. What's key is to talk without fault. Keep away from a cautious or basic comment which can make a contention raise.

✧ EDIT WHAT YOU SAY

Try not to exclaim each bad thought, particularly when you talk about delicate themes. Recall that you love the other and keep up with deference.

✧ OFFER FIX ENDEAVORS

A maintenance endeavor is an assertion or activity intended to diffuse an argument.3 This could be utilizing humor, contacting the other individual, or offering a compassionate or caring comment like, "This should be hard for you to discuss."

You could likewise settle on something worth agreeing on, such as saying, "Indeed, we have various methodologies, however we both need exactly the same thing." Or proposition indications of appreciation all through troublesome discussions.

In his book "The Seven Standards for Making Marriage Work," Gottman calls fix endeavors a distinct advantage of genuinely shrewd couples. His examination shows "the achievement or disappointment of a couple's maintenance endeavors is one of the essential variables in whether [a] marriage is probably going to thrive or fumble."

✧ FOCUS ON THE UP-SIDES

Solid and cheerful relationships offer a rich environment of energy. For each regrettable collaboration during struggle, a steady and blissful marriage has at least five positive cooperations.

In this way, attempt to offer five fold the number of positive proclamations in your conversations, including your contentions and conflicts. For instance, a cheerful couple will say, "All things considered, we truly do chuckle a ton" rather than "We never have a great time."

✧ SHARE A CARING STORY

While it could astonish you, thinking back can assist with improving your relationship. Discussions that beginning with "Recall when" and journey through a world of fond memories — about your most memorable date, your most memorable home, and interesting recollections — lead both of you back to nice sentiments. Your accomplice will be helped to remember why they fell head over heels for you in any case.

One more method for fixing and further develop your relationship is to show appreciation for specific attributes your accomplice has. Continuously add accounts to exhibit these astonishing attributes.
Since high feelings of anxiety can prompt separation, we will generally zero in on pessimistic stories and what your accomplice isn't doing. On the off chance that you're feeling undervalued, appreciate others. Retrain your consideration on association and positive stories.

These astonishing yet significant strategies above can assist you with working on your relationship. Strangely, research shows not character or similarity holds couples together. All things considered, it's the means by which a couple communicates — how they address one another, how they coexist with one another — and assuming they center around building a relationship together that makes fruitful connections.

CHAPTER SIX

CONCLUSION

Scholarly closeness is interfacing past the physical and profound level. At the point when two individuals invigorate and enhance each other's personalities for a steady and solid love climate, it implies the relationship has a high degree for scholarly closeness. Frequently couples found to have a higher level of scholarly association are supposed to be more joyful as brains of a similar worth function admirably together.

www.ingramcontent.com/pod-product-compliance
Lightning Source LLC
LaVergne TN
LVHW020526160826
845677LV00015B/3927

* 9 7 9 8 8 4 8 7 0 5 7 6 8 *